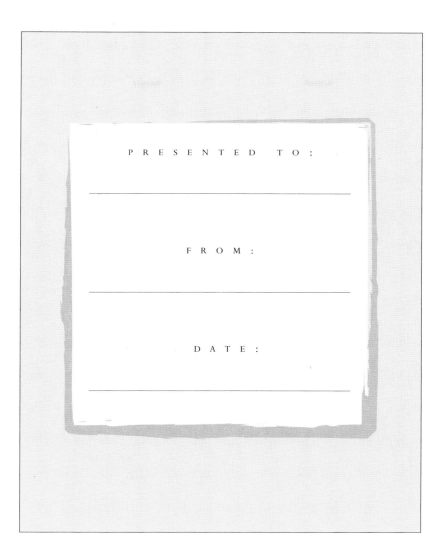

PRESENTED TO:

_____

FROM:

_____

DATE:

_____

ANNE MURRAY

Published in 2000 by Balmur Book Publishing
35 Alvin Avenue, Toronto, Ontario
Canada M4T 2A7
Tel. (416) 961-7700 Fax (416) 961-7808
Email books@balmur.com

Distributed in Canada by:
General Distribution Services Ltd.
325 Humber College Blvd. Toronto,
Ontario M9W 7C3
Tel. (416) 213-1919 Fax (416) 213-1917
Email cservice@genpub.com

Distributed in the United States by:
General Distribution Services Inc.
PMB 128, 4500 Witmer Industrial Estates,
Niagara Falls, New York 14305-1386
Toll-free Tel. 1-800-805-1083
Toll-free Fax 1-800-481-6207
Email gdsinc@penpub.com

04 03 02 01 00 1 2 3 4 5

Canadian Cataloguing in Publication Data

Murray, Anne
What a wonderful world
The book contains the lyrics to the songs on the compact disc.

ISBN 1-894454-08-1

1. Gospel Music. 2. Popular music. I. Title.
ML54.6.M87 2000   782.42164   C00-932269-8

U.S. Cataloging-in-Publication Data
(Library of Congress Standards)

Murray, Anne.
What wonderful world [text] / Anne Murray. —1st ed.
[144] p. : col. photos; cm. + 1 music compact disc.
"Includes selection of inspirational classics on compact disc."

ISBN 1-894454-08-1

1. Murray, Anne, 1945– . 2. Singers — Canada — Biography. I. Title.
782.42164/092   B   21   2000   CIP

Jacket and Interior Design: Dave Murphy / ArtPlus Ltd.
Page Layout: Leanne O'Brien / ArtPlus Ltd.

Printed and bound in Canada

"Anne Murray" is a registered trademark

Page 143 constitutes a continuation of this copyright page

THE CANADA COUNCIL | LE CONSEIL DES ARTS
FOR THE ARTS | DU CANADA
SINCE 1957 | DEPUIS 1957

*We acknowledge for their financial support of our publishing program the
Canada Council for the Arts, the Ontario Arts Council, and the Government of
Canada through the Book Publishing Industry Development Program (BPIDP).*

ANNE MURRAY

Inspired by the album
WHAT A WONDERFUL WORLD

includes a selection of inspirational
classics on compact disc

Preface

'Inspiration' means different things to different people. For me, inspiration can be a special song or a special place, like Nova Scotia.

Nova Scotia will always be home to me. The ocean inspires me, the people inspire me and I spend every summer there. Nova Scotia is the light at the end of my tunnel.

Recently I put together an album of songs that inspire me called *What a Wonderful World*. And although I've been making music and receiving fan mail for more than 30 years, nothing could have prepared me for the letters, e-mails and faxes I received after the release of this album.

Some people found themselves emotionally overwhelmed by certain lyrics; other people spoke of tunes that unleashed an unexpected flood of childhood memories. Many, many people wrote to tell me that these songs, and these sentiments, were continuing to help them through troubled times in their own lives. And their letters continue to be an inspiration to me.

May you find your own inspiration – and treasure it when you do.

Anne Murray

Every life has a plan
Though sometimes the map is out of our hands
Every day is a step
Though we may not know the reason just yet

Let there be love
Let there be light
Let there be hope in the dark of the night

For every heart that's lying in wait

Let there be love

ou are strong, you are brave
No, I couldn't even count all the ways

here's a time to be still
And let the river carry you where it will

It's a long, hard road to travel
Yes, I know what it's like when you lose your way
When the best laid plans unravel
That's when you've got to believe

*A thousand miles from home
But I don't feel alone
'Cause I believe in you*

Oh, when the dawn is nearing
Oh, when the night is disappearing
Oh, this feeling is still here in my heart

I believe in you even through the tears and the laughter
I believe in you even though we be apart
I believe in you even on the morning after

I believe in you when winter turn to summer
I believe in you when white turn to black

And I, I don't mind the pain
Don't mind the driving rain
I know I will sustain
'Cause I believe in you

I can see clearly now, the rain is gone
I can see all obstacles in my way

Gone are the dark clouds that had me down
It's gonna be a bright, bright sunshiny day

*ere is that rainbow I've been praying for*
It's gonna be a bright, bright sunshiny day

ook all around, there's nothing but blue sky
Look straight ahead, nothing but blue sky

nd in my hour of darkness
She is standing right in front of me
Speaking words of wisdom
Let it be

nd when the night is cloudy
  There is still a light that shines on me

Shine until tomorrow

Let it be

or though they may be parted
There is still a chance that they will see
There will be an answer
Let it be

Though you have to make the journey on without me
It's a debt that sooner or later must be paid
You may meet some old friend who may ask you for me
Tell them I'm coming home some day

There is no night, for in his light
You'll never walk alone

Always feel at home
Wherever you may roam

I'm on your side
Oh, when times get rough
And friends just can't be found

Like a bridge over troubled water
I will lay me down

*When evening falls so hard
I will comfort you*

I'll take your part
Oh, when darkness comes
And pain is all around

ail on silver girl
Sail on by
Your time has come to shine

All your dreams are on their way
See how they shine
Oh, if you need a friend
I'm sailing right behind

lose your eyes and think of me
And soon I will be there
To brighten up even your darkest nights

Winter, spring, summer and fall
All you have to do is call
And I'll be there
You've got a friend

*I*f the sky above you
Grows dark and full of clouds
And that ol' north wind begins to blow

Keep your head together
And call my name out loud
Soon you'll hear me knockin' at your door

When people can be so cold
They'll hurt you, yes, and desert you
And take your soul if you let them
Oh, but don't you let them

On a hill far away stood an old rugged cross
The emblem of suffering and shame
And I love that old cross, where the dearest and best
For a world of lost sinners was slain

It's all about the way things are
And not the way things might have been
How you can be ridin' in the hurricane's eye
And still have peace within

Well, I nearly searched this whole world over
Just to find me a place of rest
Where I could be myself and do
All of the things that I love best

I don't need fortune and I don't need fame
Send down the thunder, Lord, send down the rain
But when you're planning just how it will be
Plan a good day for me

Amazing grace, how sweet the sound
That saved a wretch like me
I once was lost, but now am found
Was blind, but now I see

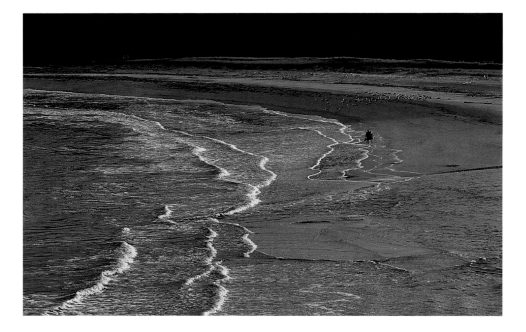

T was grace that taught my heart to fear
And grace my fears relieved
How precious did that grace appear
The hour I first believed

If there is a load you have to bear
That you can't carry, just remember I
I'm right up the road
I'll share your load if you just call me

Sometimes in our lives
We all have pain, we all have sorrow
But if we are wise
We know that there's always tomorrow

I come to garden alone
While the dew is still on the roses

*Think of your fellow man
Lend him a helping hand*

You see, it's getting late
So please, don't hesitate
Put a little love in your heart

*Put a little love in your heart
And the world will be a better place
For you, and me
You just wait and see*

ake a good look around
And if you're lookin' down
Put a little love in your heart

I hope when you decide
Kindness will be your guide
Put a little love in your heart

There's a race to be run
There's a victory to be won
Every hour, give me power
To go through

I pray no more sorrow and sadness
Or trouble will be
There'll be peace in the valley for me

Oh Lord, my God, when I, in awesome wonder
Consider all the worlds Thy hands have made
I see the stars, I hear the rolling thunder
Thy power throughout the universe displayed

ome home, come home
Ye who are weary, come home

hrough each lifetime run rivers to cross
But what if there's no lifeline and you're sinking or lost?
Just believe in your direction, let your heart explore
'Cause you can't reach new horizons standing on the shore

nd there are mountains we need to climb
But the mountains standing in our way are only in our minds

And the risk of going nowhere is the greatest risk of all
So just listen to the voice that says, I'll catch you if you fall

On the other side of doubt is faith
On the other side of pain lies strength

The journey may seem endless
When you know the road is rough
But on the other side of fear is love

Wait 'til the darkness is over
Wait 'til the tempest is done
Hope for the sunshine tomorrow
After the shower is gone

If, in the dusk of the twilight
Dim be the region afar
Will not the deepening darkness
Brighten the glimmering star?

hen when the night is upon us
Why should the heart sink away?

*When the dark midnight is over
Watch for the breaking of day*

Rise, shine, give God your glory
Rise, shine, give God your glory
Rise, shine, give God your glory
Soldiers of the cross

Or if on joyful wing, cleaving the sky
Sun, moon, and stars forgot, upward I fly

I see trees of green, red roses too
I see them bloom for me and you
And I think to myself
What a wonderful world

I see skies of blue and clouds of white
The bright blessed day, the dark sacred night

he colors of the rainbow, so pretty in the sky
Are also on the faces of people goin' by

I see friends shakin' hands, sayin', "How do you do?"
They're really sayin', "I love you"

*Yes, I think to myself
What a wonderful world*